Wherever we go,
and whatever we do,
let us live with this
remembrance in our hearts...
that we are family.

— Collin McCarty

# To My Child

## ...We may no longer live in the same house, but you're always in my heart

A collection of poems
Edited by Gary Morris

**Blue Mountain Press**®

Boulder, Colorado

ACKNOWLEDGMENTS appear on page 64.

Library of Congress Catalog Card Number: 98-30719
ISBN: 0-88396-474-0

design on book cover is registered in the U.S. Patent and Trademark Office.

*Manufactured in Singapore*
*Third Printing: April 1999*

Library of Congress Cataloging-in-Publication Data

To my child : we may no longer live in the same house, but you're always in my heart :
  a collection of poems / edited by Gary Morris.
  -- Special ed.
      p.   cm.
  ISBN 0-88396-474-0 (alk. paper)
    1. Parent and child--Poetry. 2. American poetry--20th century. 3. Adult children--
  Poetry. 4. Parenthood--Poetry.   I. Morris, Gary, 1958-   .
  PS595.P37T6    1998
  811'.540800431--dc21                                                      98-30719
                                                                              CIP

**Blue Mountain Press** ®

P.O. Box 4549, Boulder, Colorado 80306

# Table of Contents

You are still my child;
that will never change.
I will love you forever,
and that is also unchangeable.
I am here for you in the same ways
I have always tried to be.
You are my greatest accomplishment
and my source of endless pride.

Because of the distance that separates us,
I can no longer be there
for everything you do.
But I can and would enjoy
hearing about it all.
Our daily relationship is different,
but our personal one shouldn't be.
I'm as close as the phone
and as personal as a card or letter.
I have your picture on my desk
and your essence in my soul.

I loved watching you grow up;
those memories are ones I cherish.
I love the moments we have
    together now,
however short or long they may be.
Being with you has always been
    quality time,
but because of life's demands,
there has never been enough time.

I love you,
and like all parents who are
away from their children,
I miss you and think of you often.
Be safe, continue to do your best,
and remember how much you are loved.

— Ken Musgrove

# I Am Proud to Be Your Parent

It seems like it was yesterday
that I held you when you were a baby.
But time has a way of slipping past us unnoticed.
I closed my eyes for a moment,
and opened them to find you grown.

I miss those days when you spoke your first words,
took your first cautious steps,
and love and caring were all you needed.
Those were beautiful and precious times.
But now I am finding your grown-up years
are beautiful and precious, too.
You are not only my child,
you are my friend.

I never realized when you were a baby
how close we would be today.
I thought you would always be my baby,
and in a way, you are.
But as you have grown, so has my love for you.

No parent could ever feel
as close to a child as I do to you.
You are sensitive and caring, loving and giving.
You are a person whom people respect, and so do I.
I am so proud of you; please remember that.

I guess what I am trying to say is
that I am so thankful we are together,
and I am so proud to be your parent.

— Joanna Naso

# Being Your Parent
# Has Taught Me
# So Much About Life

When you were younger,
I bestowed upon you
every hope I had for the future.
Like most parents,
I wanted you to have
the advantages I never had.
I wanted you to learn from
my mistakes.
Now I see that I was wrong.
You can't learn from my mistakes;
you have to learn from your own.
As much as I would love
to pave the way for you,
you have to experience
the good with the bad
for yourself.
There's no other way to grow.
I can, however, share in
your joy, your pride,
your pain, and your sorrow —
and for that,
I will always be here for you.

— Sharon M. Boucher

# My Child,
# I Don't Ever Want You to Forget
# How Much I Love You

Sometimes parents don't make their feelings clear; they assume that their children know of the deep love they feel for them. Yet when misunderstandings occur, and things are left unsaid, it can lead to needless doubts and insecurities.

I don't ever want you to feel insecure, and I want you to remember these words I am telling you now, because they will always be current and never changing...

You are the greatest thing that ever happened to me. There is nothing I'd rather see than your smile, and nothing I'd rather hear than your laughter.

I am proud of the person you have become. And no matter what happens in your life, I have confidence in your ability to make the right choices. I love you.

— Barbara Cage

# Poems to Help My Child Be Strong Along the Path of Life

"Always keep your goodness
and never lose your love.
For then you'll be
rewarded with success
in ways you never dreamed of."

"You can be head and shoulders above the crowd.
You don't have to be a giant to be strong.
Walk tall and proud. All you have to be...
is someone people look up to."

"In the course of time, you will be reminded
that hard work gets good results and keeping
healthy is essential. Know when to work your
mind and let your body relax, and know when
doing just the opposite makes the most sense.
Being able to handle whatever life brings your
way is not a matter of coincidence."

"You've already got a good idea of what is expected of you and wished for you. One of the best things you can accomplish on life's pathway is to be a walking example of the golden rule. Don't let anyone fool you into thinking that it is worthless; it is one of the most valuable things you can do."

"You've got so many possibilities ahead! Don't be too quick to limit your choices of what to do, because you might limit your chances of unimagined joys that are just waiting for you."

"You've got a wonderful sense of humor and a good outlook on life. Let those qualities help to see you through when you're deciding where to go and you're not sure what to do."

"You've got a big heart. Keep it filled with happiness. You've got a fascinating mind. Keep finding new ways to grow. Keep yearning. Keep learning. Keep trying. Keep smiling. And keep remembering that a parent's love goes with you... everywhere you go."

— Douglas Richards

# I Will Always
# Stand by You

You are older now and
making choices of your own —
some I understand but don't agree with

But they are your choices
and I stand with you as you make them
because you are my child

Today's world is complicated —
much more so than when I was your age —
and even then my choices
were not always the wisest
so I know how difficult it can sometimes be

I salute you
for making decisions and standing by them
I am proud and confident that they are
the very best for you

I am proud of you —
a person of conviction
when the answers don't come easily
a person of strength
when others refuse to believe in you
a person of towering integrity
when you are forced to stand
in the world alone

With each new difficult choice
that you are forced to make
I want you to know
that though I may not understand
or even though I may not fully agree
I will always stand by you
and your decisions
because you are my child

But also
because you are a very special person
who knows your own heart
and follows its beat
to wherever it will take you

I love you
and am proud to say
"That's my child!"

— Wayne Jones

If I could give you the best gifts of all, they would be the everlasting kind — like sunny thoughts to lift you high above your troubles and warm rays of love and friendship always in your heart. If I could shower you with happiness each hour, I would. If I could wrap you in protective ways, I would — making sure no problem ever touched your life or displaced your joy for living. If I could take your hand and lead you securely down life's path, safely shielding you from any harm, I would.

I'd do all this for you; if only the power were in my hands, I'd give you life's best gifts. But I hope you'll see that the very best gifts are truly yours already — beginning with your independent nature and the power to choose your own way to find happiness.

All the same, I'd like for you to know and remember this within your heart: I'm close by, caring for you greatly and wishing to protect you. My best gift to you will be as it has always been: such great love for you, and my belief that you will choose your paths in life with honor and integrity, just as you always have.

— Barbara J. Hall

You have your own dreams
  and goals;
I only want to say
that you can never go wrong
if you follow your heart.
Although you are an adult now,
I hope you will never forget
the child within you.
That child will never grow up,
and will help you keep humor,
spontaneity, and trust in your life.
Others may try to place
expectations on you —
even loved ones and friends —
and you may feel under pressure
to fulfill them.
Harder still, you may perhaps
place expectations on yourself
and feel that you've failed
when you don't meet them.
But I have learned that
expectations cannot always be reached;
the best that you can ever do
is fulfill the vision you hold in your heart.
Finally, I want to say that
I will always be here for you —
to honor your growth as a person
and your journey in life
wherever it takes you —
because I love you.

— Stephanie June Sorrell

# You Will Never Be
## Too Old or Too Big
### for Me to Hold You in My Arms

All too quickly,
you were out of my arms
that held you so close,
and you were standing at my side
holding on to my hand.
All too quickly,
you let go of my hand
and placed your arms around
    my shoulders,
hugging me as the times went by.

All too quickly,
you were standing tall and strong on
 your own,
independent and self-assured,
letting me see the person you
 had become
and knowing that I couldn't have been
more proud.

All too quickly,
those days of childhood have come
 and gone,
but the memories of those times
are as clear in my mind as ever.
And because you are my child,
you will always be welcomed into
 my arms,
for you will never be too old or too big
to be held close to my heart.
You have grown up to be everything
a parent could ever dream.

— Deanna Beisser

# You Can Always Depend on Me as Your Parent and Also as a Friend

I know sometimes it's hard to ask for help. I can understand your quest for independence, that overwhelming desire to be responsible now that you're grown. But as you mature, the best wisdom can be found in the littlest things you do.

Never be too proud to reach out for help, and know that I'm always in your corner, ready and waiting to assist you. Do not think of it as an imposition, because it never is.

No matter where you go or what you need, or how far apart the miles may divide us, don't hesitate to give me a call. I'll be there when you need me, not as a parent who knows everything, but just as a person who has gone through many of the same things you are experiencing right now, and as someone who will be on your side and will listen to your point of view.

You can always depend on me. I care about you a great deal, and I'm always going to be there for you. I'll forever be on your side.

— Sarita Bradley

# What Is a Family?

A family is... the sweetest feelings ⇐ The warmest hugs ⇐ Trust and togetherness ⇐ Unconditional love ⇐ The stories of our lives written on the same page ⇐ The nicest memories anyone has ever made ⇐ Treasured photos ⇐ Thankful tears ⇐ Hearts overflowing with all the years ⇐ Being there for one another ⇐ Supporting and caring ⇐ Understanding ⇐ Helping ⇐ Sharing ⇐ Walking life's path together, and making the journey more beautiful because...

We are a family...
and a family
is love.

— Marin McKay

# To My Wonderful Child
## ...Our House Will Always Be a Home to You

You have left our house
to begin a new life of your own
I am so proud of you
and what you are doing
I want you to know that
raising you and
watching you grow up to be
who you are
has been such a pleasure —
one that I will surely miss

I realize that with your independence
a new dimension of friendship
has been added to our relationship
and I want you to know that
I am always available
if you need someone to talk to
I know you so well that
I might be able to give you
a different insight than other people could
and I want you to know that
though you are not
living in our house anymore
it will always be a home to you
full of memories and
love

— Susan Polis Schutz

I wish that I could have
   bottled your giggles
      when you were small
   and collected all of your
      handprints
         from each windowpane.

If I could have done this,
   I would take them out gently
   whenever I need to,
         and spread them across everything.
   Then, I would find such joy
         in remembering.

But I have no giggles
         or handprints
      to hold or to scatter,
   and remembering is somewhat bittersweet,
         for you are so far away from home...

...and home will never be
      the same without
      the sound of your laughter
   and the gift of your presence
      spilling out from every room.

— Priscilla Wright

# Sometimes, Families
# Have to Be Apart

Our wonderful family
is like a candle
that reflects its joy
within our hearts.

And it's like a fire
that keeps us
close and warm
no matter how long
  we're apart.

I'd give anything
to be with you more often.
But at least we'll be together
in ways that will always
shine in our lives
and that will never stop
brightening up our days.

Each time I think of you,
I promise to send you
a kiss on the wind.
And I promise I'll be counting the days
  until I can see you again.

— Marin McKay

# Your Life May Change,
# but My Love for You
# Never Will

As you have grown, my dreams for you have been locked away and replaced by your own dreams. I shared my dreams with you in hopes that yours would develop toward what is right for you. My dreams for you will be stored away like old play scripts, as you begin your performance.

I will stop being your director and begin as your coach, your mentor, your confidant... as need arises and you direct me.

I will stay one step ahead of, next to, or behind you, as you give me my cues.

I will try to think of myself as your colleague instead of your boss.

While I will always be your parent, I hope to further develop as your trusted friend.

When you fall, I will wait for you to ask for help... instead of immediately rushing in.

When you succeed, I will observe and cheer from the crowd... unless you invite me to share the stage.

When you are indifferent, I will understand that we all have times of personal questioning in our search to understand ourselves... and I will let you alone.

These are my goals, but please understand that, because I am human, my intentions will not always be fulfilled. Sometimes I will slip back into directing or even bossing you — out of sheer habit or heartfelt concern. Please know at those times that it is not because I want to dominate you, but because I love you and am needing, at that moment, to feel needed. All it will take from you at those times is a gentle, loving reminder that I trust you.

I love you, and that will never change.

— Larry Tindall

Right before my eyes, you have grown up so much on your way to becoming the special person you are today.

From a baby, to a child, to a young adult, you were full of life and filled with surprises. Trying to keep up with you has been many things: rewarding, challenging, hopeful, and fulfilling. In every one of your years, you have given me more happiness and love than most people will ever even dream of.

As a family, we have walked along many paths on our way from yesterday to where we are today. Love has always been our companion, keeping us close, even when we've been apart.

You have given me many gifts on that journey. But none are more precious than the smiles you give to my heart.

— Marin McKay

# I Will Always
# Love You, My Child

From the moment I met you
   and first saw your face,
I fell hopelessly in love with you;
   it was a fierce and protective love.
I made a solemn vow to you that day
   to love and protect you forever.

Now that you're on your own
   and not under my wing anymore,
My love for you is still as strong
   as it was then,
      even though your needs are fewer.
We've had our share of arguments,
   usually over your independence,
And we've had our share of tears,
   usually over our stubbornness.
But through it all, my love for you
   remains as fierce and protective
      as it did that first day.
I am so proud of who you are
   and of your struggle to get there.
And I just wanted to let you know...
   you mean the world to me.

— Su Pemberton

# Some Hopes
# I Have for Your Life...

May today and every day of your life bring you fresh hopes for tomorrow — because hope gives all of us our reason for trying.

May each new day bring a feeling of excitement, joy, and a wonderful sense of expectation. Expect the best, and you'll get it.

May you find peace in simple things, because those are the ones that will always be there.

May you remember the good times and forget the sorrow and pain, for the good times will remind you of how special your life has been.

May you always feel secure and loved, and know you are the best.

May you experience all the good things in life — the happiness of realizing your dreams, the joy of feeling worthwhile, and the satisfaction of knowing you've succeeded.

May you find warmth in others, expressions of love and kindness, smiles that encourage you, and friends who are loyal and honest.

May you realize the importance of patience and accept others for what they are. With understanding and love, you'll find the good in every heart.

May you have faith in others and the ability to be vulnerable. Open your heart and really share the miracle of love and intimacy.

Above all, may you be happy with yourself.

— Regina Hill

# My Child, I Will Always Be a Part of You

Have you ever wondered
who hears your sighs
and listens to your unspoken worries?
I do.
Have you ever wondered
who sees your tears
and cries for you
when life is disappointing?
I do.
Have you ever wondered
who feels your heartache
or knows the pain you hold
when your dreams fall through?
I do.
Being your parent,
I am a part of you,
and our lives,
   so joined together in spirit,
will always touch one another.

— Deanna Beisser

# I'd Love It
# If You Would Do This for Me

Every once in a while,
I want you to
close your eyes
and remember...
all the smiles
that you and I
have shared.

And, when you
open your eyes,
I want you
to smile
one more smile...
as you gently realize
that no matter how many days
or how many miles
come between us...

you and I
will
always be
as close
as close can be.

— Alin Austin

## I Want to Be
## Your Best Friend
## as Well as Your Parent

I realize that the older you get,
the less you want me to
"act like a parent" —
to reprimand, preach,
   or try to teach.
I realize that you must
   live your own life,
make your own mistakes,
and find your own solutions.

I just want you to know
that the times when I seem
    upset _at_ you
are really the times when
    I'm upset _for_ you —
because I know I have to stand aside
and watch you go through
the trials and tribulations of life
    and make it on your own.

I can see us becoming more
    like friends
than parent and child,
and I realize that a supportive
but non-interfering friendship
is more important to you right now
than a parent-child relationship.
So, because I love you so very much
and want to help you
    in any way that I can,
I am now and will always strive
    to be your best friend.

— Marion Jackel Wilson

# Thoughts of You
# Are in My Heart
# Every Day

From the moment you were born, you became the focal point of my existence. Your smile was the sunshine in my heart. Your happiness was the only treasure I sought.

And so began the great paradox of parenthood. For when your tiny hand touched mine, I knew that I had been chosen to nurture you, love you, and then give you the strength to let go.

Letting go is not easy. But I look at you now — a beautiful young adult, strong in your convictions and determined to face life on your own terms — and I still feel my heart swell with pride and joy.

My dreams for your life might not always be the same ones you seek. But one thing remains the same: your happiness will always be my greatest treasure. I know now that the true miracle of that first touch lies in one simple truth: even though your hand may slip away from mine, we will hold each other in our hearts forever.

— Nancy Gilliam

# A Family Is Love

Wherever we go,
  and whatever we do,
let us live with this
remembrance in our hearts...
    that we are family.

What we give to one another
comes full circle.
May we always be
  the best of friends;
may we always be one another's
  rainbow on a cloudy day;
as we have been yesterday
and today to each other,
      may we be so blessed
        in all of our tomorrows...
          over and over again...

For we are a family,
  and that means love
        that has no end.

— Collin McCarty

# What Being Your Parent Means to Me

Being your parent means that I have had the opportunity to experience loving someone more than I love myself. I have learned what it's like to experience joy and pain through someone else's life.

It has brought me pride and joy; your accomplishments touch me and thrill me like no one else's can. It has brought me a few tears and heartaches at times, but it has taught me hope and patience. It has shown me the depth, strength, and power of love.

Being your parent hasn't always been easy, and I'm sure I've said and done things that have hurt or confused you. But no one has ever made me as satisfied as you do just by being happy. No one has made me as proud as you do just by living up to your responsibilities.

No one's smile has ever warmed my heart like yours does; no one's laughter fills my heart with delight as quickly as yours can. No one's hugs feel as sweet, and no one's dreams mean as much to me as yours do.

No other memories of bad times have miraculously turned into important lessons or humorous stories; the good times have become precious treasures to relive again and again.

You are a part of me, and no matter what happened in the past or what the future holds, you are someone I will always accept, forgive, appreciate, adore, and love unconditionally.

Being your parent means that I've been given one of life's greatest gifts: you.

— Barbara Cage

# You've Got a Family
## Who Loves You,
## and You're Always
## Welcome Home

When words from the heart fail to make
   the desired connection,
When you're just tired of eating out and trying
   to please other people in your life,
When you need to know there's someone who
   really cares about what you're going
   through and how you're feeling,
We all need a sense of belonging sometimes.
That's the time to remember...
   You've got a family who loves you,
      and you're always welcome home.

Whether you need some understanding, an
    extra blanket for your bed, the arms of
    loved ones to hold you, a favorite dessert
    to make you feel special,
If you want someone to talk to, to listen to,
    to cry with, or just be with...
We are here and we'll never turn our backs on
    you, no matter what you're going through.
You don't have to share everything with us if
    you don't want to,
But we just want you to remember...
    You've got a family who loves you,
        and you're always welcome home.

We're here to talk about your needs, your
    hopes and plans, your disappointments,
    whatever is in your heart and on your mind.
We're not perfect, but we're here for you,
    not to judge you, but to accept you,
    to love you without condition,
    to be with you wherever you are.
So, no matter what you're going through,
    no matter what we need to do for you,
Always remember...
    You've got a family who loves you,
        and you're always welcome home.

— Donna Fargo

# For Those Times When You Need Encouragement

I know life can be discouraging at times, so I am giving you this. I want you to read it every time you feel overwhelmed, so that it may encourage you to move forward and look beyond your troubles.

If ever you feel like giving up, don't. If you think you can't do something, try. If you try and fail, then try again. If you don't, you may always wonder why you gave up so easily.

Don't let life pass you by; the only way to get ahead is to hold your head up high. Try not to be discouraged when things get in your way; just climb each mountain inch by inch, and take life day by day.

Eventually you will find the strength you had to seek, not only to scale that mountain but to reach its mighty peak.

Believe in whatever you think is worth believing in, and never stop until you feel you have done all that you can to secure your dreams. I have such faith in you, and I know that you are capable of achieving anything you want. Always remember that.

— T. L. Nash

# For You, My Child, as You Go Out into the World

Take your bright intelligence, your boundless energy, your brave spirit, your creativity, and your vast imagination. Pack all the beautiful things that make you the individual I love so much.

The people you meet in your new world and the things you see may challenge your faith, the things you believe, and the way you were taught. But if you stay true to yourself, you will meet these challenges. You will feel proud and free, and be happy, healthy, and successful.

On your journey, use your bright mind to fight wrong and dangerous ideas. Use your energy to get involved in whatever is positive and healthy. Defend your ideals. Use your creativity. See yourself doing great things, then use your imagination to help you plan how to make those dreams come true.

Take along your sunny smile, your relaxed and happy laughter, and the attitude that you are a beautiful person with the power to be true to yourself.

— Jacqueline Schiff

# To My Child...

### As a Parent,
### As a Person and
### As a Friend...

## I Am Always Here for You

When you need someone
to talk to
I hope you will
talk to me

When you need someone
to laugh with
I hope you will
laugh with me

When you need someone
to advise you
I hope you will
turn to me

When you need someone
to help you
I hope you will
let me help you

I cherish and love
everything about you —
my beautiful child
And I will always support you
as a parent, as a person
and as a friend

— Susan Polis Schutz

# When We're Apart, My Child,
# I Miss You So Much

Life is so different
when we're apart
and it will be weeks or even months
before we're together again.
I think about you
several times a day.
I wonder if you're making
new friends
and what new things
you're learning and doing.
But most of all, I wonder
if you know how much love
is sent your way every day.
You are so much a part of me,
and when we aren't together
it feels as if something
very important is missing...
        and that something is you.

— Barbara Cage

# I Always Want to Be
# a Part of Your Life

I know at times
I still tell you things
You already know.
I remind you of things
Even when I know
You haven't forgotten them.
I know it's difficult
For you to always listen to me,
Because you're not little anymore.
But when you were a child
You relied upon me
For everything.
Being needed as a parent
Is an honor
And at times
A tremendous responsibility.
I still want to be
A part of your life
Because you're so much
A part of mine.
No matter what,
I believe in you
And in all that you become,
And I love you
As you are
Always.

— Maria Shockley Erman

# Always Remember
# Who's in Control of Your Life...
# You Are!

There are so many choices
   in the world today
about where to live, what to do,
and whom to spend your time with.
But if you remember this one
   simple truth,
you'll be able to make the decisions
   that are right for you...

Never forget that you're the one
   in control of your life.
Decide on the values that are
   most important to you,
and live by them <u>always</u>.

Never compromise them
   or give them up
for another person or situation —
even when it seems as though
that's the only way to get
   what you want.
You may win in the short term
   by doing this,
but never in the long run.

You have so much potential
   and ability.
Use them wisely, and as best
   as you are able,
and everything you desire
   out of life
will be yours one day.
If you are true to
   the highest ideals
in everything you do and say
   and by how you treat others,
then success is guaranteed
   in every aspect of your life.

— Edmund O'Neill

# Just Be Yourself, and Remember... You Are Loved

To be who you are
is to be enough.
To share who you are
is to share enough.
To do what you love
is to do enough.

There is no race to win
and nothing to be proven,
only dreams to be nurtured,
a self to be expressed,
and love to be shared.

Never doubt your worth,
and always know,
without any doubt,
that you are truly valued
and deeply loved.

— Donna Newman

# I Want You to Know
# How Much I Enjoy Our Friendship

I've always loved you
and cared for you
as my child,
but since you've grown up,
we've added a new dimension
to our relationship,
that of friendship.

We understand each other
and respect each other's opinions.
We've learned that we don't
always have to agree;
we only have to accept.
Our love is one of give and take,
a sharing of hearts and lives.

You are very precious to me,
and I am so proud of you.
You've grown into a wonderful person
who still holds many of the memories
and charms of my little child,
but who also has the qualities
of a dear and exceptional friend.

— Barbara Cage

# You'll Always Have Me
## to Care About You

No matter what
life holds for you,
you'll always have me.

No one ever really knows
what life has in store,
what roads they will travel,
or how things will turn out.

It's kind of scary sometimes,
looking ahead and not knowing,
but I want you to know
that you'll always have me.
It doesn't matter where I am
or what I'm doing;
I will always take time for you.

You are a very special person to me,
and you have a place in my heart
that will always be there for you.
I want you to remember
that you will never really be alone,
because you'll always have me
to care about you.

— Beth Fagan Quinn

# To You,
# My Wonderful Child,
# I Give...

My time when you need someone
to listen or stand with you.
My heart when you need someone to care.
My support when you need to know
what a great person you are.
My faith in you,
in your goals and dreams,
and your ability to achieve them.
My perspective for when you are
confused and want another opinion.
My strength for when the path
you walk seems all uphill,
and you need to rest a bit.
My understanding when you make
mistakes or you don't live up
to your own expectations,
and you need to know that
you don't have to be perfect.

Most of all,
I give you my heart always,
for the bond between us is unconditional.

— Ruthann Tholen

# In the Words of a Parent
## Who Loves You...

$I$ hope you'll take a minute
to listen to something that needs
to be said.

It's something about being
a parent — like me,
and having a child — like you.

It's also about love — about how
it shows itself in many ways:
sometimes in hugs and happiness,
sometimes in harsh words
and hopes.

And it's about communication; about
    how we always need to build bridges
    between us and never allow walls
        to separate us. No matter what.

I want you to keep this, and to every
    now and then remember these words.
I'll always want what is best for you.

I'll try to give you roots, but I'll try
    to give you wings, too, so
    that you can feel confident enough to go
    in the directions you choose,
        but with the knowledge that
    wherever you go, you always have
    a place called home to return to
    and someone who loves
        and believes in you.
                                    — Carey Martin

When you were little,
I thought you were the most
beautiful child in the world —
like most parents do
about their children.
Now that you are grown,
I know you're the most beautiful
person — not only on the outside —
but inside where it really counts.

So many times I feel that
I let you down.
Being a parent doesn't mean
that we instinctively know
all the right things to do,
or not to do.
I wish I could go back and
do some things over, which I
would now do differently...

If I could do it over,
I would spend more time
just getting to know you
and playing with you,
and less time worrying about
the dust on top of the refrigerator
or the mess in the closet.
I would try to listen more
and be more patient.
But I can only move forward,
so I want you always to remember
that I am here for you...
Whenever you need to talk,
I'll listen.

I'm just thankful that you have
grown to be such a lovely person,
and I'm so proud that you are
my child.
I love you.

— Joy Barnett

# Your Life Is a Journey...
## Make It a
## Wonderful Adventure!

Let your life be an exploration.
Let people and places be
  a part of your life,
and experience each and every
  unique situation
with a sense of wonder and delight.
Look in all directions to seek out
the answers you long to know,
and discover the secrets that
keep questioning your heart.
Be willing to make changes and
be ready to face the challenges.
Accept the opportunities
  that present themselves,
and endure and cope with
  the difficulties
that can arise from time to time.

Remember that there is no one way
    to live your life,
but a thousand different ways for
each of us to be.
Make your life the way
    <u>you</u> want it to be
and create a lifestyle that
    brings you happiness.
Search for your true meaning in life
by devoting yourself to your ideals,
and enjoy your wonderful adventure
    through time
by making every day special.

— Deanna Beisser

## These Special Wishes
## Are Just for You...

When you close your eyes at the
end of each day, I wish you
contented and peaceful sleep.
When you are fearful or uncertain,
I wish for warmth and light
to surround you.
When you dream, I wish you
soaring images and
endless possibilities.
When you wake each morning,
I wish you the joy of anticipating
a beautiful day ahead.
When you face problems, I wish you
boundless strength and courage
to guide you.
When you walk along your path,
I wish you lasting friendships
to brighten your way.
Most of all, I wish you love...
to fill your heart
and make your world complete.

— Linda Sackett-Morrison

You may not know all that
the world has to offer...
but I know that the world
will be a better place
because of what you have
to offer it.

You may not know which path
you should follow...
but I know that you will
listen to your own heart,
for it will never lie.

You may question what you
have already accomplished...
but I know you will
never doubt what you can do.

As all of your tomorrows
open themselves to you,
never forget how proud I am
of you
and how much I love you...

yesterday, today, and always.

— Michael Coffey Tarbert

# Thank You, My Child, for All the Wonderful Memories You Have Given Me

My memories of you
   always take me back through the years...
memories of an infant
   so sweet and small and trusting,
memories of a toddler
   giggling with the joy of childhood,
memories of a youngster smiling
   and playing with friends,
memories of your teen years
   full of change and doubt and growth.
My memories of you
mark your journey from a baby to a child
and, magically, to a young adult.
I cannot believe that the time
   has passed so quickly.
And now, I see a lovely, gentle person —
   my best friend, the baby I held,
      the person with whom I shared
      secret jokes, special talks,
   laughter and victories, tears and defeats,
and gentle guidance into a world of hope.
I feared that I might have spoiled
   you many years ago,
but you spoiled me instead...
with boundless joy and soaring pride
   and a love that grew as you did.
Though miles and schedules keep us apart,
our bond exceeds distance and time.
Life is a blessing with you by my side,
   with you always in my heart.

— Darlene Helms Griffin

## My Advice to You...

Enjoy your life!
Laugh a lot.
Love a lot.
Listen to your heart,
and follow where
it leads you.
Do what you love.
Love yourself,
and share that love
with others.
This is the way
that we truly
make a difference,
add our beauty to the world,
and give something precious
to ourselves and others.
You have already
made an impression on the world.
You have touched my heart
and my life
in a way that has
forever changed me.
Thank you for coming into my life,
for forgiving any errors I made
in raising you,
and for allowing me the chance
to learn and grow with you.
I love you.

— Donna Newman

# ACKNOWLEDGMENTS

The following is a partial list of authors whom the publisher especially wishes to thank for permission to reprint their works.

PrimaDonna Entertainment Corp. for "You Have a Family Who Loves You, and You're Always Welcome Home," by Donna Fargo. Copyright © 1998 by PrimaDonna Entertainment Corp. All rights reserved. Reprinted by permission.

Sharon M. Boucher for "Being Your Parent Has Taught Me So Much About Life." Copyright © 1997 by Sharon M. Boucher. All rights reserved. Reprinted by permission.

Wayne Jones for "I Will Always Stand by You." Copyright © 1997 by Wayne Jones. All rights reserved. Reprinted by permission.

Sarita Bradley for "You Can Always Depend on Me as Your Parent and Also as a Friend." Copyright © 1997 by Sarita Bradley. All rights reserved. Reprinted by permission.

Priscilla Wright for "I wish that I could have bottled your giggles...." Copyright © 1997 by Priscilla Wright. All rights reserved. Reprinted by permission.

Larry Tindall for "Your Life May Change, but My Love for You Never Will." Copyright © 1997 by Larry Tindall. All rights reserved. Reprinted by permission.

Su Pemberton for "I Will Always Love You, My Child." Copyright © 1997 by Su Pemberton. All rights reserved. Reprinted by permission.

Deanna Beisser for "My Child, I Will Always Be a Part of You." Copyright © 1998 by Deanna Beisser. All rights reserved. Reprinted by permission.

Marion Jackel Wilson for "I Want to Be Your Best Friend as Well as Your Parent." Copyright © 1998 by Marion Jackel Wilson. All rights reserved. Reprinted by permission.

Barbara Cage for "When We're Apart, My Child, I Miss You So Much." Copyright © 1997 by Barbara Cage. And for "What Being Your Parent Means to Me." Copyright © 1998 by Barbara Cage. All rights reserved. Reprinted by permission.

Maria Shockley Erman for "I Always Want to Be a Part of Your Life." Copyright © 1997 by Maria Shockley Erman. All rights reserved. Reprinted by permission.

Donna Newman for "Just Be Yourself, and Remember... You Are Loved." Copyright © 1997 by Donna Newman. All rights reserved. Reprinted by permission.

A careful effort has been made to trace the ownership of poems used in this anthology in order to obtain permission to reprint copyrighted materials and give proper credit to the copyright owners. If any error or omission has occurred, it is completely inadvertent, and we would like to make corrections in future editions provided that written notification is made to the publisher:

BLUE MOUNTAIN PRESS, INC., P.O. Box 4549, Boulder, Colorado 80306.